PIANO • VOCAL

THE LITTLE MERMAID

W9-AQH-609

WALT DISNEY PICTURES
PRESENTS

THE LITTLE MERMAID

© 1989 The Walt Disney Company

ISBN 0-7935-0000-1

HL Hal Leonard Publishing Corporation
7777 West Bluemound Road P.O. Box 13819 Milwaukee, WI 53213

FATHOMS BELOW

Lyrics by HOWARD ASHMAN
Music by ALAN MENKEN

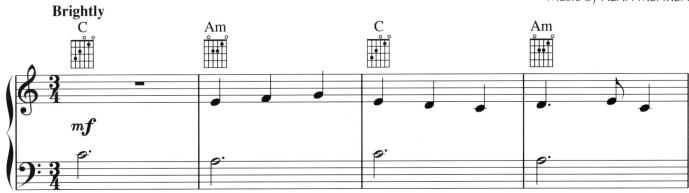

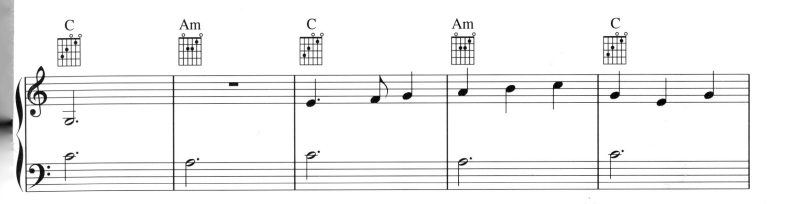

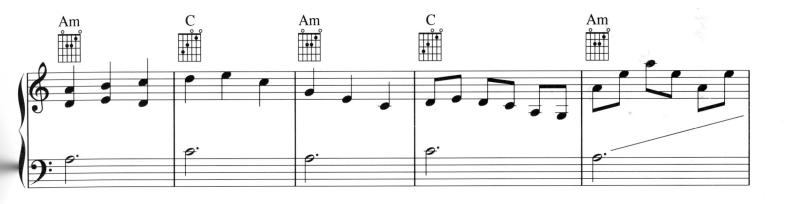

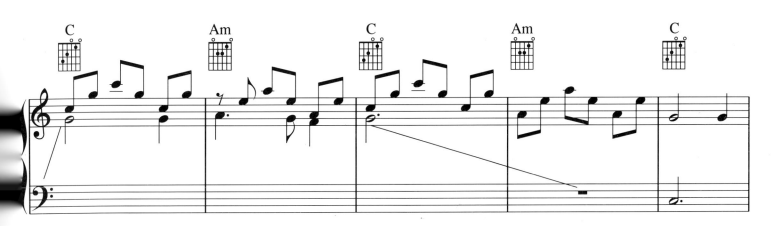

Heave,   ho.

DAUGHTERS OF TRITON

Lyrics by HOWARD ASHMAN
Music by ALAN MENKEN

PART OF YOUR WORLD

Lyrics by HOWARD ASHMAN
Music by ALAN MENKEN

UNDER THE SEA

Lyrics by HOWARD ASHMAN
Music by ALAN MENKEN

PART OF YOUR WORLD (REPRISE)

Lyrics by HOWARD ASHMAN
Music by ALAN MENKEN

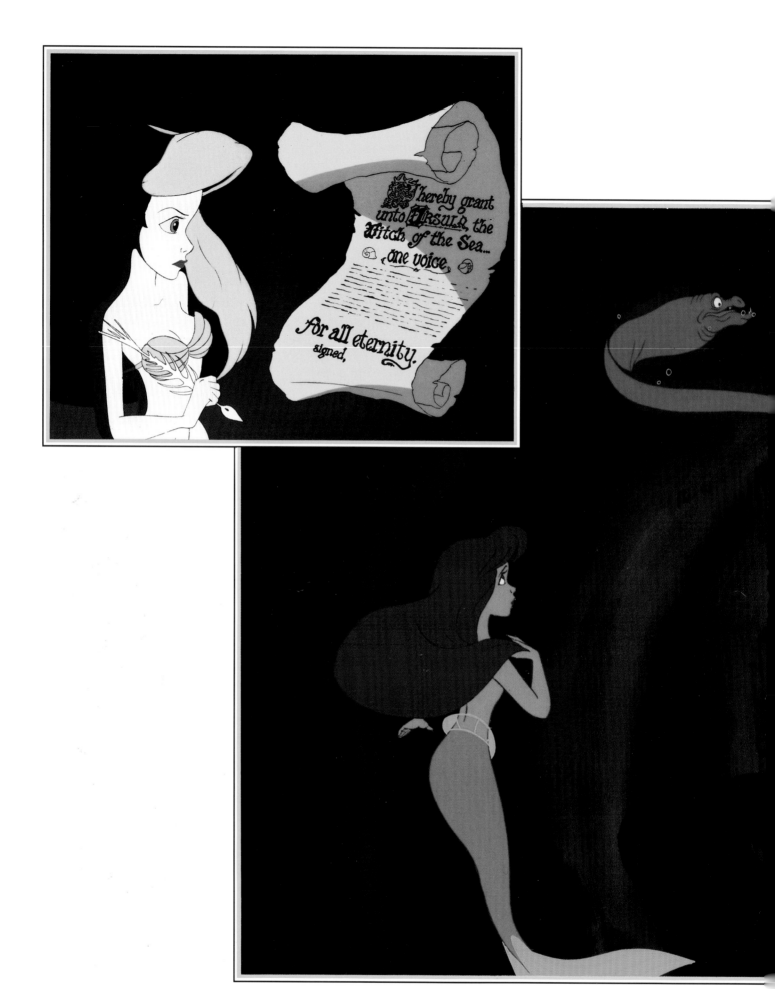

POOR UNFORTUNATE SOULS

Lyrics by HOWARD ASHMAN
Music by ALAN MENKEN

LES POISSONS

Lyrics by HOWARD ASHMAN
Music by ALAN MENKEN

KISS THE GIRL

Lyrics by HOWARD ASHMAN
Music by ALAN MENKEN

Now's your mo - ment, _____ float - ing in a blue la - goon. _

Boy, you bet - ter do it soon, _ no time will be

bet - ter. _ She don't say a word _ and she won't _